Dedicated to my Mum
She who nurtured the fire from our sparks

The Night of Starlight

Written & Illustrated by Sarah Matthews Stilwell
With additional digital elements by PawStore Graphics

Hush now.
Cuddle up snug
and tight.

I want to tell you a story
of a light
in the night.

A light

that shines out brighter

than any

candle flame.

Guilding all who
are feeling lost,

struggling,
or in pain.

A Star that is
shining still,

deep within
human hearts

- A Star that reminds us that there is light to be found in every dark.

But firstly
let us talk
of it's birth....
And
what it means
for us.
Here on Earth.

A heralding,
a happening

... A bright,
unmissable
thing....

A celestial
symbol of
a new born
King

A supernova exploding in the inky dark,

A new born star arriving to help guide us on our path.

Not glimmering, not shimmering,
no twinkle of sparks.

Just a star so radiant,
that it burnt through the dark.

So much more than
just a simple
spark.

Powerful star light, casting an arc. turning
night bright as day.

- Or so they say.

Hope in pure form,
A cosmic ray.

A diamond
like brilliance
that touched
the tips of
the hills.

Everywhere the light shone,
warmed softly
from night chills.

Seen from near,
or from a far.

A light calling to you,
no matter where
you are.

The star shone down,
Above where He lay.
A halo of magnificence.
For a baby born this day.
Oh how even the heavens did sing
Peace be upon the
new born King.

Look for it now.
It will help
guide your way.

....The very same star that shone down upon the hay.

It appears aligned
every 800 years.

A
heavenly sign
to help
rid us of our
fears.

A prophecy fulfilled,
so very long ago.

A shining,
starry reminder
to carry within us.
Everywhere
that we go...

....when our hearts feel heavy.

When we feel that we can
no longer cope....

That
there is a light
shining bright,
deep within us

It is named HOPE

Oh, how
it glitters.

An ever glowing spark.

Bright enough and
fierce enough to
banish every dark.

Guiding us home, no
matter our path.

Printed in Great Britain
by Amazon